The publishers would like to thank the following Companies for their generous support of this project

BAROSSA VALLEY ESTATES

BAROSSA WINE & TOURISM ASSOCIATION

GRANT BURGE WINES

PETER LEHMANN WINES

SOUTHCORP WINES

ST HALLETT WINES

YALUMBA WINES

THE
BAROSSA

THE
BAROSSA

PHOTOGRAPHY BY
R. IAN LLOYD

TEXT BY NIGEL HOPKINS

EDITED BY WENDY MOORE

R. IAN LLOYD PRODUCTIONS

CONTENTS

CHAPTER ONE

THE HISTORY

In a country that was built on migration – from the early convict settlers of New South Wales to an entire southern Italian village that migrated to a South Australian town – nothing was more remarkable than the European settlement of the Barossa Valley.

It had its origins in the very formation of South Australia which, unlike most other Australian states, did not begin as a convict dumping ground. Instead, its settlement was shaped by the utopian theories of the first of a long line of commercial adventurers, Edwin Gibbon Wakefield, who reasoned that instead of granting land to settlers it should be sold through the government-backed South Australian Company, using the money raised to fund the migration of free settlers.

To look at the cultural heritage of the Barossa now you might think it had been settled and shaped entirely by the Silesian refugees (from what was formerly Prussia), who have left such a strong mark on the Barossa Valley. But, there were two strands of settlement, English as well as German, that came together through the efforts of one man, George Fife Angas. He, too, was another of the adventurers who created South Australia, a social and religious idealist who was chairman of the South Australian Company, a philanthropist – when he had the money, and a fervent Baptist who was heavily involved in dissenting politics in England. At that time, there was as much religious dissent and turmoil in Britain as there was in the Prussian provinces of Silesia, Brandenburg and Posen (broadly an area east of Berlin, stretching over the border into eastern Poland).

The German Lutherans who would migrate to South Australia were known as Old Lutherans who rejected the enforced union of the Lutheran and Calvinist churches. Lutheran ministers who refused to accept the new forms of worship were suspended from office and many were imprisoned. Their congregations had to meet in secret and they, too, risked jail and having their possessions confiscated.

In 1836 – the year that South Australia was proclaimed as a British colony – one of the persecuted Lutheran ministers, Pastor August Kavel, was advised to seek out George Fife Angas in England to ask for his assistance in securing the emigration of his people to South Australia. It also brought into the picture Angas's confidential clerk, Charles Flaxman, who would play a major role in the settlement of the Barossa Valley.

Vintage was a time that involved the whole Barossa community. Here a group of women grape pickers take a break from a turn-of-the-century harvest near Marananga.

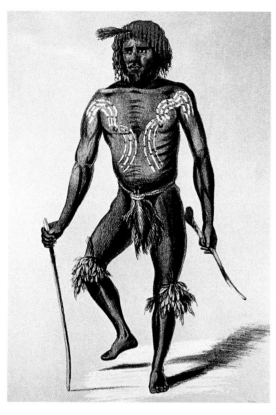

The Aboriginal population of the Barossa quickly dissipated after European settlement of the land. Noted colonial artist George French Angas captured this portrait (*above*) of one of the original inhabitants at Lyndoch in 1844. *Pictured right:* Samuel Smith (1812-1889), who started one of the Barossa's most successful and long-standing dynasties, the Yalumba winery, in 1849.

Kavel was well advised as Angas was highly sympathetic. Although he was a successful businessman, he was familiar with religious persecution in England, where nonconformists (that is, non Anglicans) were not allowed to lease land, be employed in the bureaucracy, or have a university education. However, no such constraints applied to the free settlers of South Australia where Angas and his friends in the South Australian Company had the opportunity to acquire large tracts of valuable land.

Here was an opportunity not only to practise his philanthropic Christian principles, but also to obtain hard-working, law-abiding settlers for the new colony. Angas promptly provided £8,000 to make the emigration possible, and after two years of lengthy negotiations the first shipload of Lutherans set sail from Hamburg for the eight-month journey to South Australia.

Initially they settled on Angas's land at Klemzig, outside Adelaide, at about the same time his agent Flaxman was buying up a large tract of land in the Barossa. However, Angus could ill afford this massive land speculation. He had suffered various business setbacks and was basically broke. He didn't have the money to buy the land let alone to stock it, describing the purchase as causing "the most profound grief".

Yet this was some of the best land in South Australia, exploration of which had begun in 1837, led by the famed surveyor Colonel William Light, who had planned the city of Adelaide. A more detailed exploration was begun in 1839 by the German mineralogist Johannes Menge and it was his enthusiasm for the area, which he named New Silesia, that persuaded Flaxman to buy 28,000 acres (11,660 hectares) on behalf of George Fife Angas, at a price of £1 per acre.

The Barossa was "the cream, the whole cream and nothing but the cream of South Australia", Menge raved, for it was he who first realized the huge potential of the valley. "I am quite certain that we shall see ... vineyards and orchards and immense fields of corn throughout all (of this) New Silesia, which is matchless in this colony." And so it would come to pass and Angas's fortunes were saved.

The first Lutheran settlers, now totalling around 570 in all, were looking further afield for suitable agricultural land. Flaxman offered 2,000 acres of Angas's land in the Barossa Ranges to Kavel's people who, in 1839, agreed to buy it for £10 an acre – a figure later reduced by half. It was a decision that caused a great deal of debate in the Lutheran community, and while this continued another group, led by Pastor Gotthard Fritzsche, set off to become the first German settlers in the Barossa. In 1842, they took up residence on another portion of Angas's land, 60 kilometres northeast of Adelaide, at a place he named Bethanien, now known as Bethany. About a year later Kavel and his congregation established a

similar settlement at nearby Langmeil, forming two villages between which the township of Tanunda later formed .

The scene was now set for widespread European occupation of the Barossa Valley, which eventually would drive the original Aboriginal inhabitants, the Southern Ngadjuri and Northern Peramangk, out of the region.

The first Europeans to set foot in the Barossa were impressed by its fertility, the abundance of water and its animal and bird population — the same conditions that made it ideal for Aboriginal settlement. However, on the many occasions that Europeans passed through the area they saw few Aborigines. The reason for their scarcity being the nature of their hunter-gatherer lifestyle.

Eventually the Aborigines found that their traditional hunting areas and water holes had been taken over by white settlers and they were forced to move on, some to the River Murray and others further north towards Clare.

For the immigrant Lutherans, the Barossa was a little Eden. They had no desire to live among the English in the growing coastal towns of South Australia and from the start developed closed-village settlements in which they could live undisturbed. The fact that few of them spoke English, even for several generations, raised another barrier against this Volkstum (national way of life). They also transposed their traditional housing forms and village plans — still clearly seen in Bethany — which were laid out on a typical Silesian farmlet plan called *hufendorf.*

An early view of Angas Town (later to become Angaston), soon after it was first settled in 1845, is depicted in this lithograph by George French Angas, son of George Fife Angas who pioneered settlement of the area.

The early Lutheran settlers brought with them the many different tradesmen and craftsmen they would need – one of the most important being the local blacksmith who often worked in partnership with wheelwrights and coachbuilders. Above, the smithy at Greenock around 1900, and (*right*) one of the German-style wagons that were used for everything from cartage to wedding coaches.

Farmsteads were usually grouped around a yard, with the house, sheds, stables, barn and sties enclosing a kind of keep. A smokehouse usually adjoined the kitchen, with a wood-fired baker's oven beside the kitchen fireplace. A number of these original farmhouses still remain in the Barossa, their smokehouse walls blackened by 150 years of smoke-curing bacon, ham and sausages.

House and shed walls were either stone and pug (clay paste) or timber and daub, with thatched roofs and hand-cut roof beams and door lintels. These, too, can still be seen in the Valley despite the later use of lime mortar, galvanized iron and sawn timber.

Each settlement in the Barossa was born in an atmosphere of deep religious faith and the most powerful influence in the valley, then as now, was the church – testified by the many well-used, immaculately tended churches that are still landmarks for locals and visitors alike.

Other Silesian settlements soon followed Bethany and Langmeil, such as Krondorf,

Lyndoch, Ebenezer, Rowland Flat and Light's Pass, all following a familiar farming regime that included stock grazing, orchards, vegetable gardens and, of course, vineyards. Allotments were small, ranging from three to four acres up to 40 acres, creating a mosaic of agricultural development that can still be seen today.

Not all of those early settlers were farmers, however. Also included amongst the pioneers were many highly skilled artisans such as cabinet makers, blacksmiths, wheelwrights, carpenters and tailors – all of whom added to the texture and quality of Barossa life, and to the Valley's rapid development.

In 1843 George Fife Angas had sent his son, John, to look after his South Australian business affairs: "Try to make it a moral and terrestrial paradise," he advised. Angas had continued to champion the new colony, even writing to ministers of religion throughout England in 1844 urging them to encourage emigration. "South Australia," he wrote, "holds out greater advantages in agricultural and pastoral pursuits and commercial enterprise, and possesses a more highly moral, religious and intellectual population, with Christian religious privileges, than any other of our colonies."

John Angas settled at Angas Town (soon to become Angaston) at the English end of the valley and was soon joined by a community of English migrants. Tanunda was now the Germanic end, and Nuriootpa, midway between the two, was a little of both.

The settlement of the Barossa Ranges beyond Angaston created a colonial replica of the English countryside, where large estates and huge homesteads provided havens for wealthy English

landowners – in stark contrast to the Silesian peasant farmers below.

One English migrant who arrived in 1847 was a brewery worker named Samuel Smith. He longed to own and work land – something that was denied him in England due to his non-conformist religious convictions – and it was through him and others like him that the Barossa Valley eventually became the most famous wine region in Australia.

Smith was soon living with his family on a 30-acre (12.5-hectare) block leased from John Angas which he turned into a successful garden supplying Kapunda copper miners about 30 kilometres away to the northeast. His role as

a gardener was very much in keeping with the plan the Angas family had for the region – that of a mix of farming, grazing and horticulture clustered around neat, English-style villages. Horticulture was of particular importance, and the growing of grapes for wine making was a top priority. There was a growing hope that South Australia would be able to produce wines for export of an equal, if not superior, quality to those of the old countries. Conditions were favourable as related in an optimistic newspaper account at the time: "Wherever a man has a bit of good garden ground in the colony, and can handle a spade, there he may stick in a few vines, and while he's sleeping, they'll be growing."

A coffee break for this closely-knit group of plainly dressed housewives, no doubt enjoyed with German cake, *streuselkuchen*, or honey biscuits, *honig kuchen*.

A wedding party in 1886 at North Rhine now known as Keyneton. The conservative Lutheran style of dress meant that until about 1900 even the bride's wedding dress was black, worn with a white veil and a wreath of myrtle. Wedding receptions were great affairs that often lasted two days.

It's not clear who planted the first wine grapes in the Barossa. It could have been Joseph Gilbert, a pastoral pioneer who planted vines around 1841, and whose Pewsey Vale winery by 1857 was listed among the colony's fine-wine producers. Equally, the Silesian settlers were familiar with grape growing and simple winemaking, which were as much a part of their culture as making German sausage.

Earlier, though, in 1831, the Australian wine industry was given a tremendous head start by the viticulturist James Busby, who collected a vast range of grape varieties from Spain and France and shipped them to the Botanic Gardens in Sydney. Some 362 of the 543 varieties he collected survived the journey – and some were sent to John Angas in South Australia, who passed them to Samuel Smith to nurture. Smith succeeded in establishing a number of varieties that eventually spread throughout the Barossa.

In the 1850s the discovery of gold in New South Wales and Victoria stripped the Barossa of its workforce, including Samuel Smith, but he struck it lucky and returned with enough money to buy 80 acres (33 hectares) of land on which he planted grapes and other fruit. By 1855 he exhibited his first wine at the Angaston show and by 1859, at the first Tanunda Wine Show, he

The Tanunda Brass Band, pictured in 1908, was the first of the four great Barossa brass bands and was founded in 1857. It has functioned continuously since then, playing at weddings, sports days and in street marches.

won prizes for his red table wine. That was the start of Samuel Smith and Sons, better known as Yalumba and now one of Australia's most prominent wineries – still family owned.

It is likely that wine was first made in the Barossa in 1849, but for the next ten years production remained on a small-scale domestic level. Then, an Act of Parliament provided a major stimulus by allowing an expansion of distilleries, which resulted in the area of vineyards in South Australia increasing from 750 acres in 1858 to 6,629 acres eight years later. Another boost came from the British Government's policy of encouraging the import of goods from its

colonies – including wine. As a result, import duties were relaxed enabling Australian wine to compete with that from France.

The foundations of the Barossa wine industry were laid in this period, between 1840 and 1870, when many family names became indelibly associated with the Barossa Valley: Burge, Gramp, Henschke, Lehmann, Pech, Schulz, Salter, Schrapel and Seppelt, to name just a few of the more familiar wine-industry families.

Wine entries in the local Tanunda and Angaston shows grew from just one in 1856 to 46 over the next three years. Joseph Gilbert's 1864 claret was reviewed in the *London Medical*

Winery workers take a break inside the vast Seppeltsfield winery in the early 1900s. During vintage, the Seppelts winery was reputed to provide work for more than 2,000 people, including women and children who helped with grape picking.

The Barossa's only cooperage, A.P. John and Sons, is shown here in the 1930s after it had moved into its present premises off Basedow Road. Now a fourth-generation business, it thrived in the 1920s making "one-trip" barrels exporting wine to the Empire. It is now Australia's largest cooperage. *Right page:* The imposing clock tower façade at Yalumba in 1925, which is still a focal point of the winery.

Times as "fit to rank with Hermitage" and his riesling was praised at the 1867 Paris Exhibition. The wines of the Barossa were on their way.

However, the next century would not be without some major setbacks, which almost destroyed the Barossa wine industry – although it missed the scourge of the *phylloxera* vine parasite that had devastated Europe and other Australian states, leaving the Barossa with a heritage of old vines unique in the world.

One of the first setbacks was the appeal of the Act that allowed more distilleries, which resulted in many small grape growers and wine makers leaving the industry, as well as leading to

a more specific division of labour – skilled grape growers who didn't make wine, and experienced wine makers who didn't grow grapes.

World War I brought mixed blessings, with anti-German hysteria forcing the closure of Lutheran schools and the changing of 69 place names of German origin. Bethanien became Bethany, Gnadenfrei became Marananga and Kaiserstuhl became Mount Kitchener! It wasn't much better during World War II, when German culture was suppressed, and preaching and public prayer in German banned, even though the language in the Barossa was a regional dialect that became known as 'Barossa Deutsch'.

During World War I, British interest in all things Australian increased wine exports and saw the expansion of production facilities. But it all suddenly came to a halt with the Great Depression in 1929. Again the industry rallied and the demand for fortified wines once again increased, until World War II and the end of the colonial-preference scheme sent the Barossa roller coaster downwards yet again.

It was against this background of war, racism and economic uncertainty that the Barossa entered its second century in the 1950s and over the next 50 years would become the wine-making capital of Australia.

CHAPTER TWO

THE LAND

Unlike those who would follow later, the first explorer to reach the Barossa Valley, the Surveyor General of the new colony of South Australia, Colonel William Light, didn't see a vision of orchards and vineyards. Instead, what he saw may have reminded him of the Andalusian region of Spain where he had served 25 years earlier during the Napoleonic Wars. Then, as Lieutenant Light, he had been aide-de-camp to the British Army commander, Lieutenant General Thomas Graham, who'd won a heroic victory against the French on a battleground named Barrossa Ridge.

Light was attempting to find a trade route to the River Murray that bypassed the steep Mount Lofty Ranges east of Adelaide when he reached a beautiful broad valley, bounded on its eastern side by low mountains that were a northerly extension of the same range. He named these the Barrossa Range, and the site of a future settlement at the entrance to the valley he named Lynedoch (Lyndoch) after his friend and comrade Thomas Graham, who by then had been elevated to the peerage as Lord Lynedoch.

Many believed the Barrossa was Spanish for "hill of roses", an attractive interpretation but almost certainly inaccurate. The true meaning is more likely to be "red soil", or another interpretation is "heavy soil"; either way, both are appropriate for this fertile region.

Within ten years the name had evolved to its current spelling of Barossa, due to the English pronunciation, and the broad, flat valley beneath the ranges had become the Barossa Valley – a feature that Light, when he first saw it, referred to as a plain.

"The Barossa" is an inclusive term that includes not only the Barossa Valley – the area first settled along its creeks and waterways by the early Lutheran settlers, but also the Barossa Ranges to the east and northeast of the Valley – settled largely by English landowners, many of whom created large pastoral estates, as well as the adjoining cropping and grazing land to the west and east.

The Barossa Valley proper extends as far as Greenock and Daveyston to the west, almost to Kapunda and Truro in the north, and Lyndoch and Williamstown to the south. It averages less than 400 metres above sea level and is characterized by fertile red soils.

The Barossa Ranges extend from Mount Pleasant and Springton in the south, through the hamlets of Eden Valley and Keyneton, to

With Tanunda in the foreground, the valley unfolds across the neat patchwork quilt of vineyards, towards the bare foothills of the Barossa Ranges and Mengler's Hill (*top left*), and the village of Bethany.

Moculta and Truro in the north. This area has been popularly known as the Eden Valley since the 1950s, although it was only recently formally defined as such and as a separate wine region. It has an average elevation from 400 to 600 metres above sea level, a much higher rainfall and cooler temperatures than the Barossa Valley floor, and rocky and acidic soils.

Nowhere is the division between the two sides of 'the Barossa' made more evident than the view from Mengler's Hill, in the ranges west of Tanunda. On the Valley floor below is the tapestry of many colours created by the small grape-growing allotments started 150 years ago, intersected by straight country roads leading from winery to winery, village to small town. Behind, to quote from John Heuzenroeder's poem "From Mengler's Hill", are:

> *Frost pitted hills, low, dark*
> *cracked rocks with lichen; mist*
> *on the wet trees trailing from soft gullies ..."*

The view from Mengler's Hill and other similar lookouts has been described as a 'cultural landscape' that ranges from the detail of church architecture and building materials to roadside clues about the geology and natural vegetation of the Barossa region.

You see the division clearly, too, when you approach the Valley from the Sturt Highway that skirts its western boundary. At this point you are driving through grain-growing land – wheat and barley – passing fields studded with bales of hay, with a distant view to the east of the Barossa Ranges. There's a flour and feed mill, but little evidence of winemaking.

But, as soon as you turn east through Marananga and Seppeltsfield, you're instantly into the full romance of the Barossa Valley, passing ancient bush-grown grape vines, the extraordinary winery complex of Seppeltsfield, the historic Marananga Band Hall, various bed-and-breakfast establishments, and endless vineyards: the transformation could not be more sudden or complete.

Beneath both landscapes is an ancient geological foundation that's part of the Flinders and Mount Lofty Ranges system. Movements in the Earth's crust about 500-million years ago caused this rock system to be tilted and buckled, with intense heat and pressure causing mineralization on the eastern side of the Barossa Valley and deposits of copper and gold.

One of the more obvious reminders of the Valley's geology is the extent and diversity of stone used in the construction of the Barossa's buildings. Reddish ironstone is probably the most characteristic building stone, along with dark-grey bluestone, as well as sandstone and limestone. White, pink and grey marble is probably the most important building stone in the region, which has been used both for public and domestic buildings.

The German mineralogist Johannes Menge, regarded as the father of South Australian mineralogy, found the region a treasure trove. He famously remarked that in all his 25 years of voyages and travels, he had "not met with a range of hills ... so rich in minerals as the range

This vista looks towards Jacob's Creek, now one of the most famous names in Australian winemaking. Settled by William Jacob, in the 1840s it was one of the Barossa's most significant early wineries.

from Adelaide up to Light's Pass", by which he meant the Barossa Ranges.

The earliest treasure to be found was just north of the Barossa, at Kapunda, where the discovery of copper in 1842 created huge fortunes and transformed the finances of the struggling colony. The Kapunda copper boom ended in 1879, but in the meantime, gold had been found in the Barossa Valley itself, sparking a gold rush that ended in the 1890s after some three tonnes of the precious metal had been extracted.

As Menge had predicted, the area was rich in a wide range of minerals and geological deposits, some of which continue to be mined today such as phosphate, limestone, sand and talc.

But, however inviting the Barossa landscape may have looked to early explorers and settlers, the Barossa Valley was certainly not another German or English landscape. The people who moved there had to learn firstly about the fundamental Australian conditions in which they now lived, as well as the particular characteristics of the Barossa.

Watercourses flow predominantly in the winter, when most rain falls, and underground water supplies used to irrigate vines and other crops are recharged at this time. Annual rainfall varies from 500 to 580 millimetres on the Valley floor to 700 to 900 millimetres in the higher parts of the Barossa Ranges. Average maximum

Rolling hills, gum trees and vineyards near Seppeltsfield is a reoccuring scene throughout the Barossa Valley.

During the Great Depression this avenue of 2,000 date palms was planted along the road that winds its way past Seppeltsfield, creating one of the most memorable landmarks of any wine region in Australia.

daily temperatures vary from 13°C in June to 29°C in January.

The mention of "frost pitted hills" in Heuzenroeder's poem reflects the fact that frosts occur between April and November, along with other natural hazards such as occasional summer hail storms that can devastate a grape crop in minutes.

The landscape that welcomed Colonel Light and his team of explorers had probably been strongly influenced by the previous 40,000 or so years of Aboriginal occupation. The long-standing and widespread use of 'fire-stick farming' for hunting had helped clear undergrowth and create an open parkland of grassy plains and tree-covered hills that encouraged European settlement.

Menge had described the land around Angas Park, where Nuriootpa and Tanunda now stand, as a "delightful spot of fertile land in the shape of meadows, the greatest part of which is covered with large gum trees and partly a mere grassy plain, without the least scrub."

There is still a sense of that, even though most of the handsome blue and red gums in the valley were cleared for orchards, vineyards and wheat fields. The vegetation on the slopes of the Barossa Ranges is more original with remnant woodlands of red and blue gum, pink gum, long-leafed box and rough-barked manna gum that can be seen in Para Wirra Recreation Park and Jenkins Scrub. On the higher slopes, where the soils are thinner and terrain more rugged, there is messmate stringy-bark in the Hale and Warren conservation parks, brown stringy-bark in the Kaiser Stuhl Conservation Park and dense green stands of native pines in the Sandy Creek Conservation Park.

However, one of the most distinctive trees found on Barossa roadsides is a feral import, the olive, and though in many senses it should be regarded as a weed it is, instead, highly prized as a source of high-quality olive oil that has played no small part in the resurgence of the Barossa food culture.

Like olives, fruit orchards once played an important economic role in the Barossa for more than a century, producing apples, pears, plums and apricots, but few are now in commercial production, defeated by cheaper fruit from other regions or overseas – and the greater returns now available from viticulture.

Traditional mixed farming, with beef cattle, sheep for wool production, and cereal grains like wheat and barley, continues both to the north of the Barossa Valley and to the northeast in the land originally settled by pioneering Angas and his English contemporaries.

After 150 years of settlement the Barossa now has a weathered feel to it, reflecting both a geographical and social maturity. Much of the land has undergone several generations of development: land uses have changed, the landscape has changed, yet much has remained essentially the same.

Light, Menge and Angas would still recognize their Garden of Eden. Only the Peramangk and Ngadjui Aborigines would have cause for lament.

Exotic intruders – the rough edged, thick blades of aloe (*below*) growing along Barossa roadsides are a familiar sight, along with belladonna lilies and olive trees. *Opposite page: A reminder that the Barossa Valley is not only vineyards.* Wheat fields such as this, along with sheep and beef grazing, are important additions to the local economy.

One of the joys of the Barossa is that, without much effort, you can soon find yourself on a dirt road travelling through rich farming country where grapes take their turn with lush fields of wheat and barley.

Perhaps this is what the early mineralogist and surveyor Johann Menge had in mind when he wrote: "I am certain we shall see...vineyards and orchards and immense fields of corn."

Watchful Western Grey kangaroos thrive in Kaiser Stuhl Conservation Park, 392 hectares of the rugged Barossa ranges east of Tanunda, where more than 50 native bird species have been recorded. *Opposite page:* Some of the best and oldest dry-grown shiraz grapes are grown here on the banks of Jacob's Creek, finding their way into some of the most prestigious Barossa wines.

Early this century the Barossa Valley had a flourishing fruit-growing industry. The most successful fruits grown are now apricots – such as these shown in the first stages of sun drying at Trevally Orchards – and pome fruits and plums near Angaston.

The earliest settlers remarked
on the beautiful park-like
nature of the Barossa Valley,
which now provides idyllic
settings for its wineries, farms
and tourist attractions.

Water for irrigation has always been important for vineyards and vegetable production in the Barossa Valley, although problems with salinity hampered orchard development. The most prized shiraz and grenache grapes, however, are those grown with little or no irrigation. *Opposite page:* Dense scrub and undergrowth had already been cleared from the Barossa when the first settlers arrived, possibly due to the Aboriginal use of "firestick hunting", leaving an impressive woodland of majestic eucalypts. Peppermint gums, blue and red gums filled the valleys, while pink gum, long-leafed box and manna gums could be found on the slopes of the Barossa Ranges.

New plantings are neighbours to well-established vines on a back road near Seppeltsfield, with views across the valley to the Barossa Ranges.

The Barossa Valley is home to nearly as many mixed farmers as it is to grape growers, as well a substantial number of orchardists and vegetable growers. Many mixed farms graze sheep or cattle, while cereal production is concentrated on high quality wheat and barley, with oats and legume crops in some areas.

Barossa-raised sheep for sale are inspected in a pen at a nearby auction. Sheep are raised for wool production, with some fat lamb production in the Barossa Ranges. *Opposite page:* Abandoned farmsteads such as this are testament to the harsh nature of life the Silesian pioneers faced, especially those who attempted to settle in the drier regions north of the valley around Stockwell, Truro and Dutton.

These carefully manicured
grounds and training track are
at Lindsay Park, now one of
the world's leading racehorse
studs. The property was bought
in 1851 by George Fife Angas,
one of the founders of South
Australia, and remained in the
Angas family until 1965.

THE WINE

Peter Lehmann, the doyen of Barossa winemakers, asks rhetorically: "Why do we make so many different types of wine?" Then he answers: "Because we can. How boring it would be to wake up each day and just be able to make Chateau Lafitte."

It's no arrogant boast, for the Barossa – that is the Barossa Valley and Eden Valley combined – is remarkably versatile in the range of grapes it can grow and wine styles it can successfully produce. You won't find much of dedicated cool-climate varieties such as sauvignon blanc or pinot noir, but Eden Valley riesling and chardonnay, and Barossa Valley shiraz, grenache, cabernet sauvignon and semillon rank among the best in Australia.

The Valley floor tends to produce wines that are soft, well rounded and full of varietal flavour. The flagship wine is rich, concentrated shiraz, grown from some of the oldest shiraz vines in the world. Grenache is the second most widely planted variety, whose fruit from dry-grown vines has become highly prized. The plum fruit flavour

Moment of truth for Craneford winemaker John Zilm (*left*) as he tastes his fermenting wine. Above: Nets protect some of the most valuable grapes in the Barossa in the Hill of Grace vineyard.

and aroma of ripe Barossa cabernet sauvignon has won huge acclaim for the Valley – with Lehmann's 1993 vintage winning the coveted International Wine and Spirit Competition in 1995 for the world's best cabernet sauvignon.

Semillon is the main white variety and has a distinct regional style, with substantial plantings of riesling and chardonnay, much of it blended with fruit from other regions.

The hills produce subtler, more complex flavours with Eden Valley riesling recognized as an Australian classic along with Clare riesling. Eden Valley shiraz – exemplified by Henschke's Hill of Grace and Mt Edelstone vineyards – tend to be higher in acid and more elegant than that from the Valley.

But, the Barossa wasn't always so highly valued. It's tempting, given its international fame now, to think that this was a region that had its future handed to it on a plate. But the plate was often chipped and cracked, and sometimes nearly dropped altogether. For instance, the highly-prized, dry-grown shiraz grapes from century-old vines that now fetch up to AU$5,000 a tonne were once left to wither on the vine. As recently as 1980, the average price for Barossa

The way the small, boutique winemakers do it; forking grapes from picking bins into the crusher.

shiraz grapes was only AU$200 a tonne, one-tenth of the price they fetched in 2000.

Nowhere is the rags-to-riches story more pronounced than in the history of the Barossa's most prestigious wine, Grange Hermitage. Fifty years ago, when the first vintage of the experimental wine was produced by the legendary Max Schubert, it was derided as a dry port that no-one in their right mind would buy, let alone drink. Penfold's Grange, which is produced largely from Barossa shiraz, now sells for around AU$4,000 a case.

By 1950, table wine had been made in small quantities in the Barossa for around a century, but nearly all the production went to making fortified wines – ports, sherries and flavoured dessert wines. In 1956 more than 80 per cent of wine sales were fortified, and more than half of that year's grape crush was distilled into brandy and fortifying spirit.

Max Schubert was one of the pioneers who helped change all that. In 1950 he visited Spain to learn about sherry making and on the way home stopped in Bordeaux, where he learnt about French oak maturation of cabernet sauvignon to produce longer living wines.

In post-war Australia he didn't have access to such luxuries, so he had to make do with shiraz matured in American oak, and Grange was born – setting a benchmark for a classic Australian wine style.

But the winemaker who had the most influence of all in changing the fortunes of the Barossa was Orlando's technical director Colin Gramp, the son of Orlando's former managing director Hugo Gramp, who had been killed in a famous air crash along with members of other leading Australian wine families – including Sidney Hill Smith of Yalumba.

Colin made his first table wine in 1947 – a Special Reserve Claret made mostly from shiraz with some cabernet sauvignon – and it is regarded as the beginning of the Barossa's new era of winemaking.

Gramp was an innovator who had seen the benefits of a new German technology known as cold-pressure fermentation, which he imported into Australia in 1953.

The new technology helped retain grape flavour as well as producing fruitier wines, enabling him to cause a sensation at the 1953 Sydney and Melbourne wine shows with his sweeter style of riesling, which won all the top prizes and forever changed the way white wines were made in Australia.

The introduction of more German technology in 1956 gave Gramp and Orlando its greatest coup. This was the launch of Barossa Pearl, a fruity, sparkling white wine that changed the drinking tastes of a nation that, until then, had no wine-drinking culture at all. Even by 1966, the average annual Australian wine consumption was just over two bottles per head.

Barossa Pearl was one of the most successful launches of any wine style in Australia, and was probably unmatched until the introduction 20 years later of Orlando's Jacob's Creek range of wines. It instantly captured enormous sales

– after the five-millionth bottle the company stopped counting.

Better quality wines, increasing affluence and the introduction of home refrigeration all helped the domestic wine market to grow, and with it the fortunes of the Barossa. Gradually table wine took over from fortifieds, with increased planting of grape varieties such as riesling, shiraz and grenache, and a boom in red wine consumption between 1964 and 1969 saw national consumption soar from 9.58-million litres to 25.47-million litres a year. During this period the Barossa's long winemaking tradition and its grape-processing "headquarters" role made it a trailblazer.

No other wine region in Australia could boast such a strong foundation for growth, based on some of the greatest winemaking names in the industry. Seppelts, for example, began when Silesian migrant Joseph Seppelt arrived in the Valley in 1852 and built a stone winery. His son Oscar Benno Seppelt took over the business in 1868 and developed it into one of Australia's largest wine companies.

Orlando's foundations were laid by Johann Gramp and his son Gustav in 1847 at Rowland Flat, Samuel Smith planted his first vines in 1849 calling his property Yalumba, while William Salter had bought land at Angaston in 1844, and planted his Mamre Brook vineyard, starting Saltram winery.

By the 1960s Barossa was on the brink of major change and was welcoming a new breed of winemaker. In 1961, for example, Kaiser Stuhl sponsored a young German winemaker Wolfgang Blass to come to Australia. Working under contract for Leo Buring he created

Sparkling Rhinegold, reinforcing the success of Orlando's Barossa Pearl.

But not all the expertise was imported. Roseworthy Agricultural College, whose first viticulture professor was appointed in 1895, and whose prestigious winemaking diploma was initiated in 1936, was turning out future industry leaders such as Philip Laffer, John Glaetzer and Peter Wall. In 1959 Peter Lehmann was appointed winemaker at Saltram, at the same time that riesling guru John Vickery was pioneering cool fermentation at Leo Buring.

In 1964, '65 and '68 Penfolds won the prestigious Jimmy Watson Trophy with wines predominantly made from Barossa fruit, further reinforcing the reputation of the region.

The 1960s was a period of growth and development in the Barossa that culminated in a period of investment and commercialization in the 1970s as several major companies were sold to multi-nationals – Orlando to Reckitt and Coleman (followed by a management buy out and subsequent sale to Pernod Ricard); Saltram to

The end of the vintage and autumn colours strike through the vines at Yalumba.

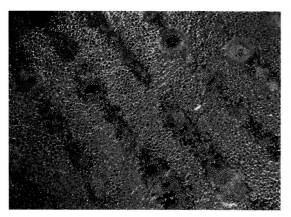

Old vine Barossa shiraz grapes in full ferment, creating a unique Australian wine style that's rich and full-bodied, with intensely concentrated fruit flavour.

Dalgety; Leo Buring to Lindeman (and subsequently Southcorp); and Seppelt to Adelaide Brewing (subsequently Southcorp).

These big companies saw wine as simply a commodity and by shifting production to lower cost irrigated regions, and failing to provide continuity of demand for grapes in the Barossa region, they created a crisis that almost brought the Barossa to its knees. It coincided with the end of the red-wine boom of the 1970s, as drinkers turned to white wine.

Meanwhile, the medium-sized, family-owned companies such as Yalumba and Henschke had continued their tradition of local purchasing. But in 1977, when there was a serious surplus of wine grapes, Saltram announced it would not be buying Barossa fruit. The following year was even worse, with prices dropping and growers facing the daunting prospect of leaving their grapes on the vine.

Enter Saltram winemaker Peter Lehmann, who decided to honour his commitment to his growers by taking their fruit and making it into wine, a brave move that made him a hero of the Barossa and, in the eyes of many, saved the wine industry. Fittingly, Lehmann and his partners named their new wine company Masterson Wines after the Damon Runyon gambler, because it was a case of win or lose everything on a single throw of the dice.

He repeated the move in 1979 and the growers survived, but the Barossa was out of favour – a bitter period that reached its nadir in 1986 with the infamous vine-pull scheme initiated by the South Australian government to rid wine regions of unwanted red and white varieties. The idea was to do away with redundant varieties such as sultana, palomino and doradillo in the Riverland and replace them with new varieties such as cabernet sauvignon. This did occur, but many old shiraz and grenache vines were uprooted in the process.

This destruction of some of the Barossa's old vine heritage was compounded by a period of rural subdivision that saw much prime vineyard land in the Barossa taken over for housing developments. This would eventually be addressed in the late 1980s when a residents' association won a freeze on subdivision and the retention of viticultural land.

By the early 1980s wine writers were wishing the Barossa farewell and a leading Roseworthy wine lecturer, Dr Richard Smart, was predicting that the Barossa Valley would cease to be a significant grape-growing region by 2001 with its crush declining to 9,000 tonnes. Fortunately he was wrong and in 2001 the Barossa crush was nearer 60,000 tonnes.

The Barossa survived thanks to its close community culture, the stoicism of its German settler heritage – growers' belts were just pulled tighter, and the development of a number of remarkable small- to medium-sized wineries that breathed new life into Barossa Valley wines.

Fifth-generation winemaker Grant Burge and Ian Wilson bought Krondorf winery in 1978 and promptly won a Jimmy Watson Trophy. Two years later St Hallett Old Block Shiraz was launched by winemaker Robert O'Callaghan who, in 1984, started his own winery, Rockford, and in the same year, Charles Melton Wines and Heritage wines were opened. In total, 12 new wineries opened during the 1980s.

Winemakers started paying growers higher prices, helping to protect vineyards from the vine-pull scheme and re-establishing regional pride by valuing Barossa-grown fruit. The new spirit entering the Barossa was exemplified by a group of wine makers, led by O'Callaghan, who started the first Barossa Classic Gourmet Weekend in 1985, a promotional event that was hugely successful in bringing together the food and wine of the Barossa. And, it hasn't looked back. Wineries, and their customers, started recognizing the value of 100 per cent Barossa Valley wines and started paying prices that ensured growth and gave growers a measure of security they hadn't ever really experienced. Now major wineries such as Orlando and Southcorp make a point of highlighting Barossa fruit in their premium wines and provide grower-incentive schemes to ensure the continual supply of low-yield, intensely flavoured, old-vine shiraz and grenache grapes.

Bottle-fermented sparkling reds and traditionally made, basket-pressed and open-vat-fermented red wines have become the hallmark of Barossa quality. And, it hasn't hindered innovation, either, with enormously experienced winemakers such as Jim Irvine making a world-beating merlot — probably just to show that he, and the region, could — very much in the spirit of Peter Lehmann.

The renaissance of the Barossa has continued and the accolades have kept coming. Stephen and Pru Henschke were awarded International Winemakers of the Year at the London International Wine Challenge in 1994, the same year that Yalumba won Sparkling Wine of the Year. Peter Lehmann Wines repeated its world champion success with its 1989 Mentor Blend at the 1996 International Wine and Spirit Competition. And in 1996 Penfold's Grange was named US Wine of the Year by the prestigious *Wine Spectator* magazine.

The Barossa has also led Australia's spectacular wine-export growth. Orlando's

The Yalumba winemaking team, continuing a 150-year-old tradition, with winemaking director Brian Walsh and winemaker Louisa Rose seated in the foreground.

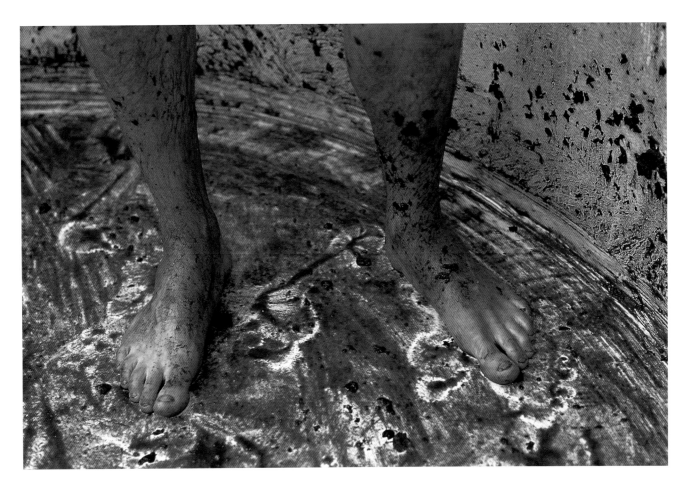

Jacob's Creek, the most popular Australian brand for over a decade with more than 4.3-million cases sold in 2000, sells at least 80 per cent of its production in more than 50 export markets – making it the number-one wine brand in markets such as the United Kingdom, New Zealand, Ireland, Scandinavia and much of Asia. In 1993 Orlando Wyndham was rewarded for its international efforts, being named Australian Exporter of the Year.

Expansion continues unabated in the Barossa, with more than 55 wineries – mostly small and family owned, and around 600 independent grape growers listed in 2001. Huge processing facilities, such as the Beringer Blass complex on the Sturt Highway, have been built that will be capable of crushing 75,000 tonnes a year – considerably more than the entire Barossa production in 2000. Vineyard plantings have shown a steady overall increase, although riesling production has decreased. However, premium shiraz is expected to double in production in the first few years of the new century.

Last word, as with the first, goes to winemaker Peter Lehmann: "The Barossa is having so much success and so it should," he says. "It's God's own country and has established itself as one of the great wine regions of the world. Margaret (his wife) is convinced that this was the original Garden of Eden."

Opposite page: Hand made wines at Rockford, where the traditional basket press is still an integral part of the winemaking process. Winemaking can also be a messy business (*above*) when it's time to clean out the fermenters.

The awesome Penfolds barrel
store at Nuriootpa frames chief
red winemaker John Duval,
who is responsible for icon
wines such as Penfolds Grange.

Opposite page: Some of the oldest shiraz vines in the world are grown here in the Hill of Grace vineyard at Gnadenfrei, near Moculta. Planted around 1880, they produce very low yields of intensely flavoured fruit for Henschke's renowned Hill of Grace wine. At the same time, new plantings are needed to expand and regenerate the Barossa's vineyards. Ross Koch (*above*) cultivates between rows of newly planted vines at Rowland Flat.

The distinctive grid pattern and alignment of the land survey by William Jacob in 1841 simplified navigation on the valley floor. From the air, the individual nature of the vineyards and small landholdings becomes evident, creating a colourful patchwork.

Opposite page: Bethany Winery is nestled high on a hillside overlooking the hamlet of Bethany, where the Schrapel family has been growing grapes for more than 140 years. The winery was started only in 1977. The view from Seppeltsfield (*above*) looks towards Greenock Creek and Gnadenfrei.

Hand picking old bush-grown vines near Tanunda is slow and hard work for the pickers. *Opposite page:* Modern trellising enables mechanical harvesting, here being done at night by Orlando at Rowland Flat.

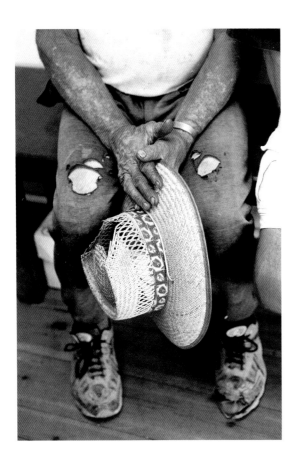

Barossa legend Peter Lehmann (*right with glasses*) with his growers at the Lehmann winery weighbridge outside Tanunda. In the late 1970s, when a grape glut led to growers' contracts being dishonoured, Lehmann took the gamble of buying the grapes and turning them into wine – a move many believe saved the Barossa from disaster.

Using restored winery equipment that many would regard as antique, winemaker Robert O'Callaghan
at Rockford Winery takes a hands-on approach to making wine that has achieved a worldwide
reputation. *Right:* O'Callaghan wheels a traditional basket of grapes ready for pressing.

74

Shiraz juice spurts from the crusher at John Zilm's Craneford winery, near Truro, and is pumped into the fermenter (*right*).

Opposite page: Traditional techniques of coopering are still used by A.P. John & Sons at Tanunda, the Barossa Valley's only commercial cooperage. Central to the making of good quality casks is the process of heating the unfinished cask over a steady fire of oak off cuts, which opens the pores of the timber. *Above:* Ancient shiraz vines in the Henschke Mt Edelstone vineyard are protected from birds by nylon netting.

State-of-the-art facilities at the new Beringer Blass winery, where winemaker Wendy Stuckey is working her way through 120 individual white wines prior to making decisions on blending.

Opposite page: Fifth-generation Henschke owner and winemaker Stephen Henschke checks progress on the ferment of his 2001 Hill of Grace shiraz in traditional, open-concrete fermenters at his Keyneton winery. Several wineries, including Penfolds (*above*), have in-house coopers who repair and refurbish barrels each year.

The winery buildings of the Barossa range from the very humble to grandiose. Some of the most impressive were constructed at Seppeltsfield (*above*), in particular this magnificent three-storey Victorian bluestone building. In a different style, but just as imposing, is the Seppelt Dorrien building (opposite page), built at Seppelt's Siding in 1911.

Surrounded by liquid history, Saltram winemaker Nigel Dolan reflects on the heritage of a wine company that can trace its history back to the 1860s, when William Salter planted his first vineyard near Angaston.

CHAPTER FOUR

THE PEOPLE

Time has slowly mellowed the differences in heritage that so marked the early years of the Barossa Valley.

After five generations a common sense of "being Barossan", based on a mutual understanding of similar ideals – regardless of their origins – is perhaps the most defining characteristic of the region's people today.

At the same time, an infusion of outside blood over the past 30 years has brought new talents and professionalism to the Valley, preventing it from becoming some quaint, ethnic backwater – not that this would really have been possible, given the international focus of the wine industry during this period.

But at the heart of the Barossa is still a tradition of hard work, a sense of the seasons and the soil, and that means its grape growers, like septuagenarian Max Gersch, are still its backbone. His youngest shiraz vines are as old as he is, and the older vines are "at least 100".

Max is one of an elite group whose grapes go into Australia's most prestigious wine, Penfolds Grange, sourced mostly from the Barossa. "A few years ago," he recalls, "no grape grower really talked about quality or knew where their grapes ended up. For me it's quite a thrill to know

that we're growing good quality grapes and contributing to the industry in some way."

It's probably unfair that it is the winemakers who have become the superstars rather than the growers of the fruit on which they depend, but some of the winemakers truly deserve that status because of the broad contribution they've made to the success of the Barossa.

Mention has already been made of the renowned pioneer winemaker Peter Lehmann. These days control of Peter Lehmann Wines rests with his son Doug Lehmann, but to see Peter in his element you just have to mosey along to his weighbridge during vintage where he's still in charge of the scales (now fully computerized).

"The Barossa has never had *phylloxera* (a vine parasite), war or prohibition," he declares with gruff authority, "which is why it's been able to have 150 years of uninterrupted grape growing." If the Barossa were to have its own benign version of Bacchus, he would probably look and sound a lot like Lehmann.

But he's not the only winemaker or vigneron who has built the Barossa. Robert Hill Smith, managing director of Yalumba, is another. He has managed to keep Yalumba intact as Australia's largest surviving family-owned winery, even

The antique shops of the Barossa Valley are renowned for their treasures. Dulcie Phillip models some fashions of yesteryear at her Tanunda shop Best of Both Worlds.

Robert also has a major interest in one of the Valley's leading restaurants, Vintner's, and sponsors the annual Yalumba Harvest Market, managed by his wife Annabel during the Vintage Festival. It's an echo of his mother Helen's involvement in the Barossa's food culture through her role in the establishment of Angaston Cottage Industries.

The newer breed of Barossa winemaker is exemplified by Robert 'Rocky' O'Callaghan who started Rockford Wines in 1984. His Basket Press Shiraz and sparkling Black Shiraz have become highly prized benchmark wines, but his contribution to the region has been more profound than that, as the leader of a residents' association in 1987 that achieved regulation of regional development and protected rural land.

He's a traditionalist whose wine continues to be "hand made" — literally, as his vines are pruned by hand, his grapes shovelled into the basket press and the skins shovelled out again. An ancient stationary engine still powers the winery equipment — a scene that enchants both visitors and the network of young artisan winemakers that Rocky has spawned. That network now includes star winemakers such as Michael Waugh at Greenock Creek, David Power at Torbreck, Peter Schultz at Turkey Flat and Chris Ringland, whose Three Rivers shiraz sells in the US for more than US$300 a bottle, more than the legendary Penfolds Grange.

The Barossa's traditions live on in daily life — quite literally with the butcher, the baker and the candlestick maker.

Graham Linke is typical of the traditional butcher still to be found in the valley — Linke's in Nuriootpa and Schulz in Angaston are the most

The bakers of the Barossa Valley are famous for good reason, and none more so than the Apex Bakery in Tanunda where Brian 'Nipper' Fechner continues to bake with a wood oven and 80-year-old traditional recipes.

enduring a tricky time in the late 1980s when he orchestrated a buy-out by his immediate family of the other shareholders, and subsequently switched from fortifieds into table wines. As for the future, Robert admits that "there's a lot of wine in the world and the question for us as a family business is what are we going to do to survive ... in this generic global wine lake."

famous, each still maintaining smokehouses for their bacon, hams and chickens, and smallgoods such as mettwurst, kasslers, *lachsschinken* (smoked pork fillet) and *jaegerbraten* (hunter's loaf – slow-roasted pork belly stuffed with beef, pork and veal mince).

Graham is a third-generation butcher whose smokehouses operate 24 hours a day, seven days a week, with fire carts on wheels burning red gum and mallee roots, and oak or red gum sawdust to create the smoke – the exact formula remains a trade secret. He admits it's a "lot of work, but very rewarding," with his smoked products now in great demand from metropolitan consumers around Australia.

The Valley is blessed by having a number of fine bakers, with Tanunda's Apex Bakery leading the way by continuing with traditional recipes handed down since the bakery was built in 1924 by Albert Hoffmann. It was bought by Keith Fechner (known as 'Chiney') in 1948, and is now run by Chiney's three sons – Brian ('Nipper'), David and John. They wanted to modernize, "but Dad wouldn't have it," Nipper says. "He insisted we stick to the traditional recipes and natural ferments. Thank goodness we did. It's kept us on the straight and narrow."

Apex bread takes six hours to make, compared to 30 minutes for a modern bakery – the ferment alone takes four hours. All of the bakery's products – including its famed *bienenstich*, German cake and honey biscuits, continue to be made just the way Albert Hoffmann made them.

Products such as these have helped to create a food culture that has been developed by former restaurateurs such as Maggie Beer, whose successful fine foods business draws on ingredients and traditions that are uniquely Barossan. She's been joined in the food business by daughter Saskia who sells guinea fowl as well as ducks, geese, free-range chickens, milk-fed lamb and yabbies (freshwater crayfish).

It's a food culture that is now being turned into a brand name, rather like the French appellation system. In time, the term 'Food Barossa' may well have the same cachet as 'Bresse chicken'.

Jan Angas, who runs her own Farm Follies business producing splendid preserves and chutneys from local produce, is one of the driving forces behind Food Barossa, which has formed a formidable network of Barossa producers – Weich's egg noodles, Zimmy's Barossa Valley produce, Oxley farm cheese, Bartonville dill cucumbers, Angaston olive oil, and so on.

One of the most endearing characteristics of Barossa people is their strong sense of community and at the heart of this is still the church.

"It's easy to be overly romantic about the role the church still plays in the Barossa," says Pastor David Gogol in his Bethany Lutheran church, "but it is still at the core of the community, albeit a smaller core than it once was."

One suspects that Pastor Gogol, who grew up in the Barossa, would have gotten

Adding value to the Barossa's formidable produce is one of the goals of Jan Angas, who is helping to lead the way with her own Farm Follies' brand.

on well with Pastor Gotthard Fritzsche, who established the Bethany congregation. A former winemaker turned preacher, he's unafraid of pushing his congregation to stay in touch with changing times.

"Traditional Barossa people still work six days of the week and pray on the seventh," he says. "They're very conservative, but when they play,

they really play. They work the hardest and play the hardest. This is how they have developed a toughness as a community that's given them the capacity to hang in when the going is hard. God plays an important part in that – they have an unshakable faith."

The newcomers to the valley have brought with them a sense of renewal and regeneration – and the energy and skills to bring about positive change. Case in point is Margaret Lehmann, a former teacher and librarian who came to the valley in 1970. She was part of a strong residents' association that brought about important planning changes, has worked hard to upgrade local library services, is chair of the Food Barossa committee, and has helped guide community development of one kind or another, although it's a role she downplays. "There are lots of like-minded people in the Barossa," she says. "You're never doing these things on your own. When people here feel there is a good idea that will benefit the Barossa, there is an extraordinary degree of unselfishness."

Another newcomer who has made her mark is vintage festival manager Barbara Storey. New York born, with a background in event organizing, she honeymooned in the Barossa in perfect spring weather and decided she could live there. Now she organizes at least 1,000 volunteers every two years when they put on the vintage festival in a massive exercise that bears out the truth of Margaret Lehmann's words. "It's a way of keeping traditions alive," Barbara says, "and the only way to do this is by sharing them."

That sense of old- and new-world traditions is also seen in the way artists and craftspeople have adapted in the Barossa.

Legendary winemaker Wolf Blass is wearing the colourful robes that designate him as one of the Barons of the Barossa – a wine brotherhood started in 1975 to preserve the traditions of the Barossa.

David Nitschke is fifth-generation Barossan from a family of grape growers and farmers, who became a policeman and then turned to wood carving and cabinet making. It wasn't a conscious decision to pick up the mantle of the Barossa's traditional German furniture makers, but he's very aware of the connection. David is well-known for his religious sculptures and woodcarving, and has exhibited widely.

And then we come to the candlestick maker, Harry Hennig who, at his Marananga workshop, keeps the old Barossa traditions of the smithy alive at his coke-fired forge where he makes everything from candlesticks to wrought-iron gates and balustrades.

Fourth-generation cooper Peter John is another craftsman who has had to move with the times whilst maintaining the traditional skills of his family company, A.P. John & Sons, started by his great-grandfather in the early 1890s. Back when Peter started as an apprentice in 1976 the company was making only 100 new barrels a year; in 2000 its capacity was more than 20,000 barrels a year, making it one of the world's top 15 coopers and Australia's largest.

As always, it is the artists who have the keenest eye for the community around them. Although there are a number of Barossa artists with national and international reputations – including painters Sabine Diesen and Allan

The master of wine marketing Bob McLean, who played a major role in putting the Barossa onto the world wine map, briefly at rest in the cellar of his St Hallett Winery.

Hondow, and sculptor Paul Trappe — they don't form a close artistic community as such.

Painter and sculptor Rod Schubert, whose forebears arrived with the first boatload of Silesian settlers in 1842, is perhaps the most acclaimed Barossa artist, even though the valley itself is not the focus of his paintings. "It's too orderly and green, but as a place in which to live and work it's the best in Australia," Rod admits, adding: "There's also a social environment in which you are left alone to do what you will, without any pressure to prove yourself. Anywhere else and I'd be considered weird or eccentric."

Cartoonist David de Vries has lived in the Barossa with his family for just over ten years,

following his partner Glenn Lumsden who'd been on his way to live in Adelaide when he discovered the Barossa instead.

As highly successful cartoonists responsible for Batman and Phantom comics, published in *Mad* and *Star Trek* magazines, they represent the influence of the new world in the Barossa. But, as David points out, it is the Barossa's old world values and traditions that attracted them.

It seems appropriate that the Barossa was born as part of the utopian ideal that established South Australia in the 1830s under the benevolent guidance of Edwin Gibbin Wakefield and George Fife Angas. Unlike elsewhere, the Barossans have kept that ideal alive.

Church and music are two fundamental influences on Barossa daily life. *Opposite Page:* A warm welcome is extended at the 130-year-old Tabor Lutheran Church in Tanunda, while (*above*) members of the Marananga Brass band, formed in 1924, perform during the Barossa Vintage Festival.

Fifth-generation Barossan painter and sculptor Rod Schubert, pictured here in his Mengler's Hill studio, has won an international reputation mostly for his highly distinctive style of painting, but also for the wine labels he's created for wineries such as St Hallett and Peter Lehmann.

Opposite page: The creative index of the Barossa jumped several notches with the arrival of international cartoonists David de Vries (*left*) and Glenn Lumsden. They draw Batman and Phantom comic strips and their work is published in well-known magazines such as *Mad* and *Star Trek*. German-born painter Sabine Deisen (*above*) works in a more traditional impressionistic style from her Tanunda studio.

Opposite page: Modernist stone sculptor Paul Trappe, who works in both the Barossa and Germany, is dwarfed by one of his majestic granite sculptures. His works in granite and marble can be seen in the Barossa, as well as in Europe and North America. The Tanunda Liedertafel, pictured at rehearsal (*above*), continues a tradition of musical and singing groups in the Barossa. Founded in 1861, it is still a favourite Barossa attraction.

Opposite page: The family tradition of preserving and smoking meats is continued by several butchers in the Barossa, including Graham Linke, pictured in the smokehouse behind his family's butchery in Nuriootpa. The fine details of the smoking process remain a tightly held trade secret. Memories of another once-vital tradition in the Barossa, that of the smithy, are kept alive by Barry Gardner (*above*) in the Doddridge blacksmith shop in Angaston, established in 1873 and maintained now as a working museum.

Innovative winemaker Charles Melton (*above*) surrounded by bunches of pedro ximines and muscadelle grapes drying in a tin shed that will go into his desert wine Soto di Fero - which literally translates as "under the iron". *Opposite page:* Fifth-generation, Barossa-born wood carver David Nitschke continues a tradition of craftsmen woodworkers in the Barossa whose work is highly prized by today's collectors.

Opposite page: Dill pickle master Steve Zimmerman with his family who turned their business into a regional success story. Chef, author and food entrepreneur Maggie Beer (*above*) started a small farm shop with her husband Colin selling pheasant pâté, saw it grow into one of Australia's most renowned restaurants, and now has placed the Barossa firmly on the culinary map with her range of Pheasant Farm products.

CHAPTER FIVE

THE ATTRACTIONS

Opposite page: **Cycling makes an ideal way to get around the Barossa Valley, with special cycling routes to follow such as the Mawson Trail.** *Above:* **An ancient red ironstone wall is covered by creepers at Langmeil Winery.**

Some images of the Barossa are indelible: the avenue of 2,000 date and fan palms at Seppeltsfield planted during the 1930s, and its mini-village of 19th-century stone buildings; the Orlando arch over the main road at Tanunda; Peter Lehmann gruffly greeting his growers at his winery's weighbridge; crisp pasties being taken out of the Apex bakery's 80-year-old wood-fired oven; slabs of bacon hanging in the smokehouse of Schulz's butchery; 800 happy revellers, arms linked and swaying as they roar "Ein Prosit" at one of the vintage festival big-band nights — and the rumpled quilt of vineyards sloping down from the Barossa Ranges.

The Barossa Valley has been so well defined as Australia's premier wine-producing region it's tempting to think that's all it has to offer. That would be enough, of course, for most people. But, in fact, there's very much more to this 30-kilometre-long valley, a little over an hour's drive north of Adelaide, that never fails to surprise or delight.

The Barossa is driven by its soil, its climate, its people and its seasons. The vines themselves, of course, are the most vivid barometer. But then there are the dill cucumbers and fields of purple salvation jane in late summer, quinces and pink bella donna lillies in autumn and wild olives in the winter months.

The butchers and bakers in the Barossa Valley come from the same tradition as the grape growers. Butcheries, such as Schulz's in Angaston, is renowned for its garlic mettwurst, fritz, smoked bacon and hams, while at Linke's in Nuriootpa, their German-style stuffed and smoked pork products are legend.

The Apex bakery in Tanunda provides a good reason to find yourself eating a freshly-baked pastie before breakfast. It still uses the 1924 wood-fired "Scotch" oven that's fired up at 5 a.m, two hours before the bread goes in. The bread recipes here are still the same as they were in 1924. So it is, too, with the German cake and *bienenstich* ("bee sting") yeast cake, cream-filled with toffee almond and peanut topping. At Christmas there is stollen, filled with marzipan and dried fruit.

Much of the local produce makes its way onto the menus of local restaurants, some of them nationally renowned such as Landhaus in Bethany, where chef Sandor Palmai cooks exquisite dishes such as caramelized duck and shallot broth with sherry-braised chicory and swede dumpling.

At the other end of the scale are brilliantly simple places such as Seasons of the Valley in Angaston, with homemade duck-egg pasta and a very stylish version of a pie floater. In between are places such Vintners Bar and Grill in Angaston, which has given a modern flavour

Foals take a look at the world outside the stable block at the historic Angas Park horse stud.

to what was an institution in the Barossa, again with lots of local produce; and the 1918 Bistro and Grill in Tanunda, where you can dine on local produce in front of a cosy winter fire.

Several of the more than 50 cellar doors also have small cafés — such as St Hallett, Saltram or Zilm's Café at Craneford Wines, and if you're in search of a gastronomic "oom-pah-pah" there are places offering leberkase, bockwurst, jaegerbraten or kassler, all with sauerkraut and potato salad, of course.

The cellar doors are a main attraction with nearly 2.5-million cellar-door visits recorded in 1999, emphasizing the value of wine tourism in the Barossa. They range from simple, rustic premises at the smaller family-owned wineries to sophisticated showcases such as those at Seppeltsfield, Orlando, Lehmann and Penfolds.

They provide a wonderful opportunity to taste the full flavour of the Barossa, including wines that haven't been widely released or are in short supply. With many smaller wineries there may also be a chance to meet the winemaker. There's no obligation to buy, although it would be courteous if you do — with efficient transport arranged for purchases.

The Barossans have a tradition of working hard, but when they decide to have fun they do so loudly, such as at the annual Tanunda Brass Band Contest each October, when brass bands that are the pride of local communities come together. Visitors can sit in on rehearsal nights, such as the Marananga Brass Band on Tuesdays.

The valley's strong musical traditions are continued also by the Tanunda Liedertafel, a male voice choir formed in 1861, which stars on occasions such as the Melodienacht held

each May. Again, visitors are welcome during practice every Tuesday night downstairs in the supper room at the rear of the Tanunda Soldiers Memorial Hall.

More music happens at the Barossa International Music Festival, held every spring, when world-renowned soloists, ensembles and orchestras perform in the local wineries, churches and cellars. At a more popular level, Barossa Under the Stars attracts big-name singing stars each February for a concert under summer skies.

Then there's the Vintage Festival every two years, starting on Easter Monday, when outsiders join the locals in an enthusiastic celebration of

the Valley's splendid repast of food and wine. This is an extraordinary event that involves almost every corner of the Barossa, together with thousands of its residents.

Taking to the back roads will lead you past neat, sturdy, white-painted storybook churches whose steeples mark the spiritual centres of this still deeply religious Lutheran community. The music tradition continues here also, with some famous locally built pipe organs and enthusiastic church choirs.

The pioneer history of the region can still be seen in the humble slab-sided barns and pug cottages, steep-roofed farmhouses and houses built from locally-quarried ironstone and

Angaston, which was first settled in 1842, and is now a modern regional centre, was strongly influenced by the pioneer Angas family, after whom it was named, and developed predominantly as a British rather than a German town.

HOLDEM

Sheep dogs have played a special role in Australia's farming communities, something that is celebrated by the highly trained performances of Norm's Coolies troupe of sheep dogs.

sandstone. One of them, Luhr's Cottage at Light's Pass, has been restored to reveal the traditional German style of 150 years ago.

Can you stay in these places? Yes, you can at many of them. The range of accommodation in the Barossa is huge: from simple roadside cottages to luxurious rooms in places such as The Lodge, a former home of the Seppelt family, or the Novotel Barossa Valley Resort.

The valley's natural heritage also goes on show in its several conservation parks – Kaiser Stuhl, Para Wirra and Sandy Creek are among the most popular, providing picnic settings, bushwalking trails and havens for wildlife such as kangaroos, possum, echidna and a range of

colourful birdlife. For some, a simple picnic at the top of Rifle Range Road, on the slopes of the Barossa Ranges, is as close to heaven as they need to get.

The Barossa is well placed as a base for travellers wanting to look further afield in South Australia. A good start is Kapunda, a mere 20-minutes' drive away, the site of Australia's first copper mine in 1844 and still a thriving township. A fascinating walking trail leads visitors back into the town's prosperous history, past heritage buildings wearing characteristic "Kapunda lace" wrought-iron work on their verandahs, and past the remains of old mine workings, shafts and tunnels.

Burra, about 40 minutes' drive further north, also owes its early fortunes to copper and was once a vastly wealthy frontier mining town. Its mining heritage and the memory of its early Cornish, Welsh, English and Scottish miners have been carefully protected – especially in the town's many old miners' cottages that have been sensitively restored and are now used for visitors' accommodation.

It leads into the mid-north of South Australia, much of it low, rolling country clad in wheat and barley, its colours subtle and its profile undramatic. But catch it when the fields are in full ripeness, or when the harvesters are carving highways through the corn, or even when it's been reduced to a bare stubble, and you'll see a gentle beauty that goes to the heart and soul of South Australia.

Some of it is big gum country, especially as you head north towards the Clare Valley, about an hours' drive from the Barossa. Here are wineries side by side with grand old eucalypts and merino sheep studs that, in their day, virtually defined the nation's merino flock.

Winemaking began here when Jesuit migrants from Austria, fleeing religious and political persecution, settled in the Clare Valley and established the region's oldest existing winery at Sevenhill in 1851, initially to produce sacramental wine.

"Because we have farming next to vineyards, there's a lovely visual contrast in summer," says Brother John May, a Jesuit for 50 years and chief winemaker at Sevenhill since 1972. "There's a very country-like feel to the wineries here. We don't want to be like the Barossa. We want to keep it small and personal."

The best way to discover The Clare, as the region is still known, is on bicycle or foot along the Riesling Trail, a twenty-six kilometre section of the former Spalding to Riverton railway. Its southern terminus is the former Auburn railway station, now finely converted as Mount Horrocks's cellar door, with its northern terminus behind Leasingham winery in Clare.

Or you can go east from the Barossa to the River Murray, following in the footsteps of the early explorer Colonel William Light.

Mannum, also about an hours' drive from the Barossa, is the birthplace of the River Murray paddle steamers and there's still the beautifully restored PS *Marion*, 100 years old and still with a regular cruise schedule, the PS *Murray Princess* and the *Proud Mary*.

This is where the Barossa's winemakers take time out with wooden boats, river cruisers and houseboats, a place where the great river's romantic past lives on and is easily shared.

The Barossa has all the contemporary trappings a visitor could want, from breathtaking helicopter flights over its vineyards to the most modern winemaking technology, sophisticated food and accommodation, multilingual tour operators, and so on.

But it's also a bit like stepping through the mirror in *Alice in Wonderland*: behind the modern façade is another quite wondrous world, which lives and breathes, and is nourished by the people of the Barossa Valley.

Taking a break from feeding the masses on Tanunda Town Day, during the Barossa Vintage Festival, these community-minded citizens try their own hot dogs.

Opposite page: Lutheran church steeples are a distinctive feature of the Barossa landscape. This one belongs to the Zion Lutheran Church at Gnadenberg, a name meaning "hill of grace" – which was the name that was given to a small vineyard planted opposite the church in 1880, now made famous by the Henschke winery. Church cemeteries record the region's German heritage with monuments such as this angel (*above*) near Bethany.

Breakfast amid the vines...luxurious bed and breakfasts such as Lindsay House provide the mainstay of accommodation facilities in the Barossa, often providing sumptuous country breakfasts and complimentary bottles of wine.

Opposite page: A row of agapanthus in flower frame the worn textures of a red ironstone building at Langmeil winery. A lakeland setting (*above*) provides grand surroundings for the Yaldara Estate winery.

To the north, beyond the Barossa, the wine tradition continues in the Clare Valley. *Left:* Brother John May, chief winemaker at Sevenhill Cellars, established in 1851 by refugee Jesuit migrants, tastes barrel samples in his historic cellars. David Hay (*above*) gives a cooking class at the top-rated Thorn Park Country House near Clare.

Opposite page: Gawler, on the south western edge of the Barossa Valley, is a world-class centre for gliding, attracting hundreds of glider pilots from around Australia and overseas each year. *Above:* The grandeur of the days when sheep ruled the country, or almost: George and Sally Hawker at the historic Bungaree sheep stud north of Clare.

The River Murray is the lifeblood of much of South Australia, a major source of water for irrigation and farming (*right*) and a magnificent refuge for humans and wildlife alike. Many people enjoy hiring houseboats (*above*) and cruising past majestic sandstone cliffs such as these.

Shades of the Mississippi are evoked in the most luxurious way to cruise the Murray – on board
the *Murray Princess* paddlesteamer. Meanwhile, on the banks of the Murray (*above*), a Sunday
afternoon picnic party of jovial Italians provides music and much amusement.

Scarecrows that once had a practical purpose to protect crops from birds provide an amusing addition to the landscape each Vintage Festival, when neighbours try to outdo each other with their whimsical creations.

The Barossa knows how to host grand events, such as splendid wine dinners during the Vintage Festival (*top*), performances by visiting musical groups such as this string quartet (*above*), or simply having a darned good time, such as when the locals turn out in the Tanunda Show Hall (*right*) and dance to the melodious tunes of their famous brass bands.

GRAPE SPITTING CHAMPIONSHIPS

12.3... ...AY

$1... ...Y

Spon...

Ford ...ALLEY ...FORD ...ty. Ltd.

Opposite page: The Yalumba Harvest Market, held during each Vintage Festival, sees Yalumba Winery turned into a huge market and picnic ground where local produce can be enjoyed with relish. *Above:* A game anyone can play – and many do – the grape-spitting championships held during Tanunda Town Day during the Vintage Festival.

Everyone turns out for the Vintage Festival parade, with a jazz band leading the Penfolds float (*above*). After the parade, it's down to the Tanunda Oval for the fair (*right*) and an afternoon of feasting and frivolity.

Locally produced crafts and produce find ready buyers at a street stall (*top centre*) during Tanunda Town Day, while gaudily-dressed clowns provide a laugh at the fair. Vintage cars (*above*) provide another link with history in the Vintage Festival parade. *Following page:* The vintage is over, the grapes have been picked and are in the barrel, the vine leaves turn golden, red and brown as autumn approaches. Another season has ended in the Barossa.

SUGGESTED READING

Vineyard of the Empire: Early Barossa Vignerons 1842-1939, *by Annely Aueckens, Geoffrey Bishop, George Bell, Kate McDougal, Gordon Young, published by Australian Industrial Publishers Pty Ltd.*

The Barossa - A Vision Realised, *by Reginald S. Munchenberg, Heinrich F.W.Proeve, Donald A. Ross, Anne Hausler, Geoffrey B. Saegenschnitter, Norris Ioannou, Roger E. Teusner, published by Lutheran Pubishing House.*

Explore the Barossa, *published by State Publishing South Australia.*

Barossa Journeys - into a valley of tradition, *by Norris Ioannou, published by New Holland Publishers (Australia) Pty Ltd.*

Barossa Food, *by Angela Heuzenroeder, published by Wakefield Press.*

A Dwelling Place at Bethany, *by H.F.W.Proeve, published by Openbook Publishers.*

Barossa-Eden Valley Classification 1947-1999, *by Peter Fuller, Brian Walsh and the Barossa Winemaking Technical Sub-Committee, published by the Barossa Wine and Tourism Association.*

Australian Geographical Indication Application - Barossa and Eden Valley regions, *published by the Australian Wine and Brandy Corporation.*

A Concise History of Australian Wine, *by John Beeston, published by Allen & Unwin.*

Wine Atlas of Australia and New Zealand, *by James Halliday, pubished by Harper Collins.*

A History of South Australia, by R.M.Gibbs, *published by Southern Heritage.*

Discover Australia Wineries, *edited by Peter Forrestal, published by Random House Australia.*

Adelaide 1836-1976 - A History of Difference, *by Derek Whitelock, published by University of Queensland Press.*

ACKNOWLEDGMENTS

The photographer and writer would like to thank the following for their generous help in the preparation of this book: Jan Angas, Maggie Beer, Wolf Blass, Leo Broadbent, Arthur Dabernig, Sabine Deisen, David deVries, Rachel Dittrich, Nigel Dolan, Col Donohue, John Duval, Peter Fuller, Annette Gilbert, Pastor David Gogol, Valmai Hankel, Sally & George Hawker, David Hay, Stephen Henschke, Robert Hill Smith, Brenda Ho, Stow Kentish, Yin & Paul Knight, Dean Kraehenbuhl, Ross Kraft, Phillip Laffer, Peter & Margaret Lehmann, Graham Linke, Robert Linn, John & Colleen Little, Joan Lloyd, Glen Lumsden, Vivienne McKenna, Bob McLean, Charlie Melton, Reg Munchenburg and the Barossa Valley Historical Society, Gerri Nelligan, David Nitschke, Robert O'Callaghan, Pam O'Donnell, Selena Oh, Marilyn Pattison, Dulcie Phillip, Oliver Portway, Barry Salter, Rod & Tia Schubert, Michael Seeliger, Michael Speers, Barbara Storey, Wendy Stuckey, Bruce Thiele, Paul Trappe, Brian Walsh, Richard & Lyn Woldendorp and John Zilm.

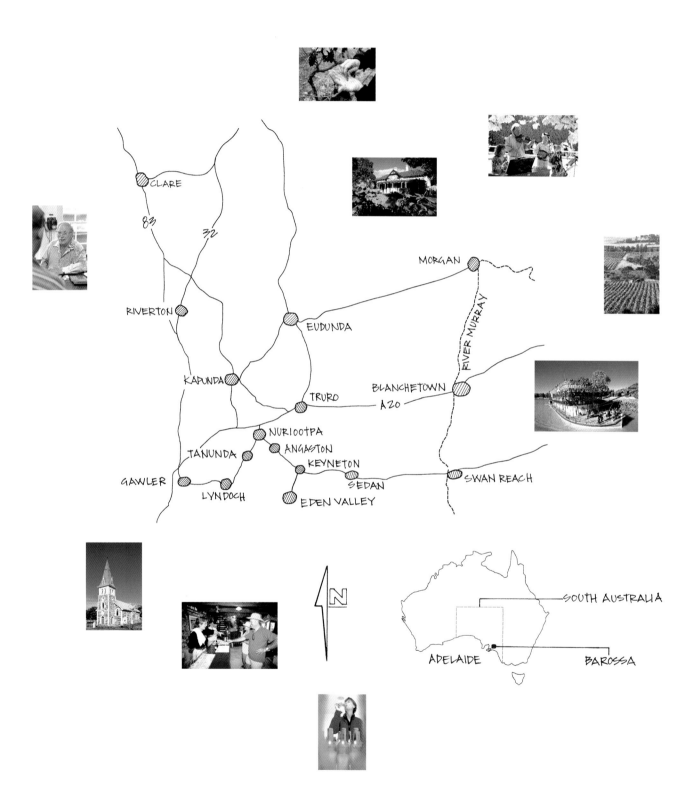

CLARE

83

32

RIVERTON

EUDUNDA

MORGAN

KAPUNDA

TRURO

BLANCHETOWN

A20

RIVER MURRAY

NURIOOTPA

ANGASTON

TANUNDA

KEYNETON

GAWLER

LYNDOCH

EDEN VALLEY

SEDAN

SWAN REACH

N

SOUTH AUSTRALIA

ADELAIDE

BAROSSA

Photography by: R. Ian Lloyd
Text by: Nigel Hopkins
Edited by: Wendy Moore
Design Concept : Yolanta Woldendorp
Layout: Canopy Design

The Barossa - Australian Wine Regions
was first published in 2001 by:
R. Ian Lloyd Productions Pte. Ltd.
5 Kreta Ayer Road, Singapore 088983
Tel: (65) 227-9600 Fax: (65) 227-9363
Email: library@rianlloyd.com.sg
Website: http://www.rianlloyd.com.sg

Historical photo credits: Page 12 & 18 courtesy
of Tanunda Framing & Pix. Page 14, 15 (top), 16,
17, 19, 20, 21, 22, 23, & 24 from the Barossa
Valley Historical Archives. Page 15 (bottom) & 25
courtesy of Yalumba Wines.

Map on Page 140 by Kevin Sloan.

This book is available for bulk purchase for sales
promotion and premium use from
R. Ian Lloyd Productions Pte. Ltd.

Distributed in Australia by:
Tower Books Australia
PO Box 213, Brookvale
NSW, 2100, Australia
Phone: (61) 2 9975 5566
Fax: (61) 2 9975 5599

Printed in Singapore using the computer to plate
process by Tien Wah Press Pte. Ltd.
ISBN No. 981-04-4313-7
10 9 8 7 6 5 4 3 2 1